SKELETONS! SKELETONS!

All About Bones

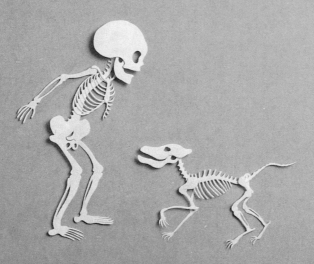

by Katy Hall • illustrated by Paige Billin-Frye

A Platt & Munk **ALL ABOARD BOOK**™

My thanks to consultant Dr. Thomas M. Kleuser, orthopedic surgeon—K.H.

Text copyright © 1991 by Katy Hall. Illustrations copyright © 1991 by Paige Billin-Frye. All rights reserved. Published by Platt & Munk, Publishers, a division of Grosset & Dunlap, Inc., which is a member of The Putnam & Grosset Book Group, New York. ALL ABOARD BOOKS is a trademark of The Putnam Publishing Group. THE LITTLE ENGINE THAT COULD and engine design are trademarks of Platt & Munk, Publishers. Published simultaneously in Canada. Printed in the U.S.A. Library of Congress Catalog Card Number: 90-82153

IBSN 0-448-40108-8 (papberback) A B C D E F G H I J
ISBN 0-448-40109-6 (library) A B C D E F G H I J

What are big and small,
and help you stand tall?
Bones!

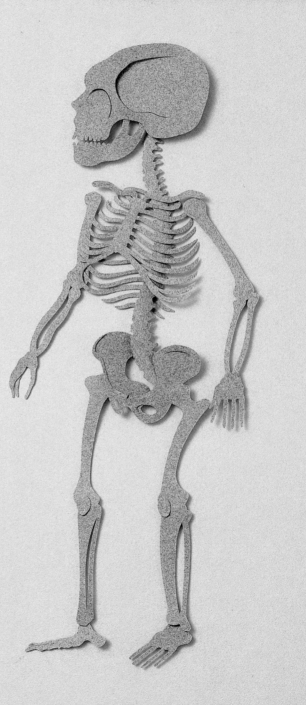

You are full of bones. Some are little, like your finger bones. Some are big, like your hip bones.

Each of your bones is connected to at least one other bone. All of your bones together make up your skeleton. Your skeleton gives you your shape. Without your skeleton, you would collapse like a rag doll.

What do babies have more of than adults?
Bones!

A new baby has more than 300 bones. They are not as hard as a grown-up's bones. They are made mostly of cartilage, which is like bone but softer. Your nose and ears have cartilage inside.

As a baby gets bigger, many of its bones grow together and get harder. A grown-up has 206 hard bones.

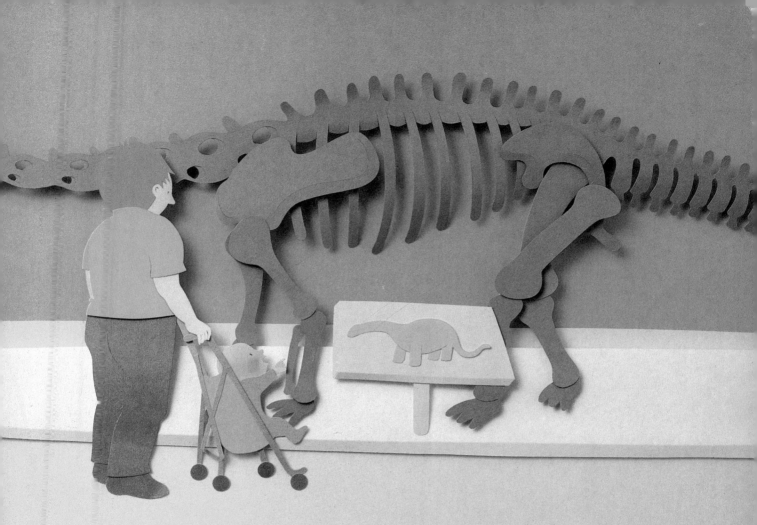

The dinosaur bones you see at a museum are dead bones. But your bones are not dead. The outside part of your bones is made mostly of minerals. Rocks are made of minerals, too. Your muscles are attached to the hard outside part of your bones. Inside your bones is spongy material called marrow. Here, new blood is made for your body. Blood vessels go in and out of your bones. Your bones have nerves and can feel pain. The bones inside you are very much alive!

What helmet can you never take off?
Your skull!

Your skull is like a hard helmet. It protects your brain when you bump your head. Your skull also protects your eyeballs and the tiny bones of your inner ear.

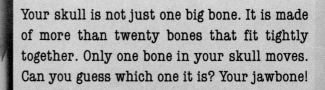

Your skull is not just one big bone. It is made of more than twenty bones that fit tightly together. Only one bone in your skull moves. Can you guess which one it is? Your jawbone!

What cord plugs into your skull?
Your spinal cord!

An electrical cord is filled with small wires. The wires carry electricity from one place to another.

Your spinal cord is made up of many delicate nerves. Like wires, the nerves carry messages back and forth between your brain and all parts of your body.

The vertebrae are joined together by flexible ligaments that work like rubber bands so that you can bend way over and touch your toes. Or you can arch the opposite way and do a backbend.

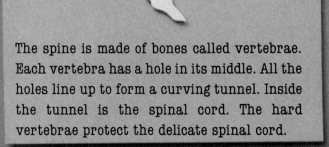

The spine is made of bones called vertebrae. Each vertebra has a hole in its middle. All the holes line up to form a curving tunnel. Inside the tunnel is the spinal cord. The hard vertebrae protect the delicate spinal cord.

What cage is inside you?

Your rib cage!

The bars of the cage are your ribs. Inside the rib cage are your lungs. Before you blow up a balloon, you take in a big breath. Your lungs inflate with air. They get bigger. When you blow out your breath, the air goes from your lungs into the balloon. Your lungs get smaller. When you breathe, muscles lift your ribs up and out of the way of your lungs. Besides protecting your lungs, your rib cage also protects your heart, stomach, and liver.

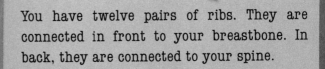

You have twelve pairs of ribs. They are connected in front to your breastbone. In back, they are connected to your spine.

What bow can you never untie?

Your elbow!

Your elbow is where your large upper-arm bone connects to the two thinner bones in your lower arm. Places where bones connect are called joints. Your elbow is a joint—a hinge joint. It lets your arm move back and forth like a hinge on a door. Your knee is a hinge joint, too. It is where your large thigh bone connects to the two thinner bones in your lower leg, or calf.

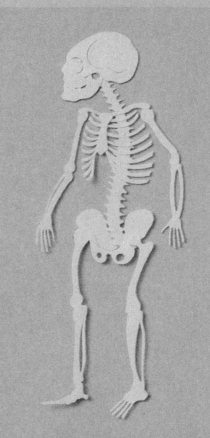

There are two hundred joints in your body. Fifty-six of them are in your hands.

Your shoulders have ball-and-socket joints. So do your hips. In this kind of joint, a "knob" at the end of one bone fits into a "dish" at the end of another bone.

Your shoulder joint lets you move your arm in a big circle. This comes in handy when you are winding up for a pitch!

Our skeletons give us our human shape. They support and protect our insides. They help us stand, sit, walk, run, bend, and do all the things that humans do.

But humans aren't the only ones with skeletons. Most animals have skeletons, too. Their skeletons are different from ours because their ways of life are different. Every kind of animal has a skeleton that is suited to the way it lives.

Sea creatures have skeletons designed for living underwater. A lobster's hard shell is its skeleton. A skeleton on the outside is called an exoskeleton. It protects the lobster from its enemies.

Fish skeletons have long, flexible spines. This allows fish to swim easily by swishing their tails from side to side. Instead of limbs, fish have bony fins. They use the fins underneath their bodies to paddle in the water. The fins on top of their backs keep them from rolling over in the water.

This is the skeleton of a sea creature that can grow to be 110 feet long. That's the length of three school buses! Its jawbone is so big that if it were set on end, the world's tallest basketball player could walk under it without ducking! The bones of its spine alone weigh more than ten whole cows! Can you guess what animal it is?

If you give up, try this see-through trick: Hold this page up to a light. Now can you see what creature the skeleton belongs to? Try this trick on any page where you see this.

The blue whale!

The blue whale may look like a fish, but it isn't one. It cannot stay underwater all the time the way fish do. It must come to the water's surface to breathe air.

Scientists have just learned from fossils of whale bones that whales were once land creatures and had four legs! But in time, whales gave up their life on land. They began life in the sea. Over millions of years, their front legs changed into flippers, and their back legs disappeared.

This skeleton belongs to a creature that is good at playing hopscotch, and even better at playing leapfrog. Do you know what it is?

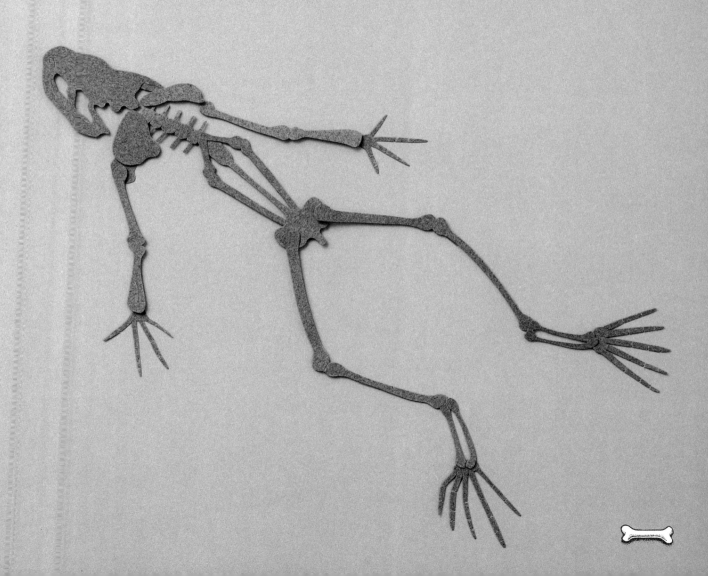

A frog!

Notice how the bones of a frog's hind feet are the same length as its calf and thigh bones. When a frog jumps, first the thigh straightens out, then the calf, and then the foot. This gives a frog great leaping power, which is useful in escaping the many animals that would like to have frog legs for dinner!

Imagine how big your feet would be if they were as long as your thigh and calf bones!

Some animals are long. Some are short. But this animal can be measured only in inches. Can you guess what it is?

A snake!

It can be measured only in inches because it doesn't have any feet!

A snake doesn't have legs or hands or arms or shoulders, either. A snake skeleton is simply a skull and a long spine, with a pair of ribs attached to each vertebra. This is just the right bone structure for slithering through desert sand and twisting up jungle trees.

Some snakes, like the python, have unusual jawbone joints that can unhinge. The python can open its mouth wide enough to swallow a pig!

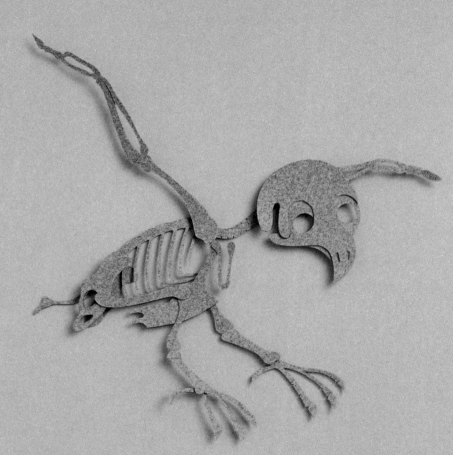

Birds need to be lightweight in order to fly. Their bones are different from the heavy bones of other animals. Many bird bones are hollow, like straws. Others have built-in air pouches. And birds don't have teeth, which are heavy. Instead they have lightweight beaks.

The main bones in a bird's wing are like the three long bones in a human arm. Feathers grow from the skin stretched around these armlike bones.

This bird doesn't give a hoot about staying home at night. Who is it?

An owl!

An owl is a mighty night hunter. Its skull has big eye sockets to protect its huge eyes, which are designed to take in as much light as possible. Even when it seems pitch-dark to us, an owl can see a tiny mouse on the ground. The feathers on its powerful wings are especially soft. This lets an owl fly silently through the night in search of its prey.

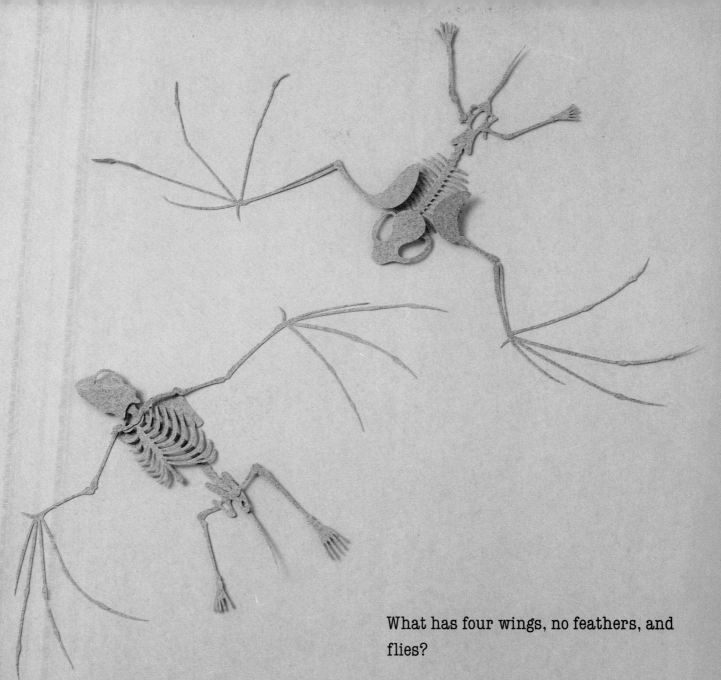

What has four wings, no feathers, and flies?

Two bats!

Like birds, bats have lightweight bones. But bats are not birds, and a bat wing is very different from a bird wing. The bones in a bat wing are like the bones in your hand. Thin skin stretches between its "finger" bones. The biggest kind of bat has a wingspan of six feet! Some bats can fly at speeds of up to thirty-two miles per hour.

Many animals that live on land have skeletons that are alike in many ways. Their skull "helmets" protect their brains. Their flexible vertebrae protect their spinal cords. Their rib cages protect their lungs, hearts, stomachs, and livers. Each of their four limbs has one large sturdy bone connected to two thinner bones. These bones are connected to the bones of a hand or foot. But within this pattern, there are many differences.

What animal <u>knows</u> with its <u>nose</u>?

A dog!

A dog's skull is large in the nose—or snout—area. It provides plenty of room for all the sensitive nerves that give a dog its keen sense of smell.

Because its sense of smell is so good, a dog does not depend on eyesight as much as humans do. For this reason the eye sockets in a dog's skull are not very big.

Like its relative the wolf, a dog has long, strong leg bones for running fast. It also has big, pointed teeth for killing prey.

Here's the skeleton of an animal that loves springtime! Can you guess what it is?

A kangaroo!

For a kangaroo, anytime is spring-time! The strong bones of its back legs are designed for springing. If an enemy is chasing it, a kangaroo can leap thirty feet in a single bound!

A kangaroo doesn't need its short front limbs for getting around. Instead it uses them for holding things and for playing "boxing" games.

When it wants to rest, a kangaroo can lean back against its sturdy tail.

Do you know what key hangs upside
down?

A monkey!

A tail is just a continuation of an animal's spine. Tails help animals that walk on all four feet to balance.

Muscles in this spider monkey's tail let it wind around a tree branch and are strong enough to hold the monkey while it hangs around!

The group of animals most like humans are the apes. Human and ape skeletons have many things in common. And they are both missing one thing that monkeys have: tails!

When is a tail not a tail?
When it's the end!